CONTENTS

LOOK FOR THE SEA MONSTER

Look for the plesiosaur logo in boxes like this.
Here you will find extra facts, stories and other
items of interesting information.

LIFE IN THE SEA

Experts believe that the first life began in the seas about 3500 million years ago. Nearly 700 million years ago, the oceans were home to animals such as jellyfish and worms.

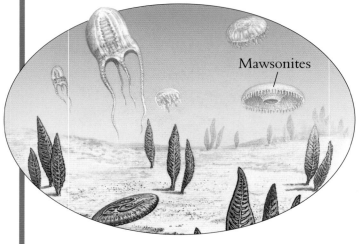

Mawsonites

▲ One of the first animals on the Earth was the *Mawsonites* jellyfish.

Some of the world's oldest animal remains have been preserved in rocks at Ediacara, Australia. This area was once a warm, shallow sea, and about 680 million years ago, its waters were filled with all kinds of strange animals. These included the *Mawsonites* jellyfish and *Dickinsonia*, a flat worm-like creature that grew about 13 cm long.

Mawsonites floated in the sea, eating particles of drifting food, while *Dickinsonia* crawled on the seabed.

Dickinsonia

remains found at Ediacara

▶ The story of life in the sea stretches back many millions of years. However, most kinds of animal lasted only a few million years before dying out.

'Cambrian Explosion'

Anomalocaris

Eurypterus

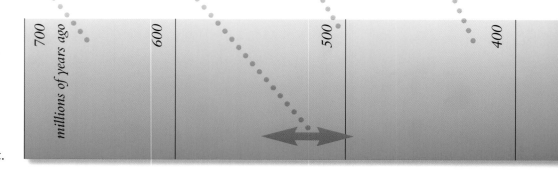

millions of years ago

700

600

500

400

PREHISTORIC ANIMALS

SEA MONSTERS

MICHAEL JAY

Chrysalis Children's Books

First published in the UK in 2003 by
⑥ Chrysalis Children's Books
an imprint of Chrysalis Books Group Plc
The Chrysalis Building, Bramley Rd,
London W10 6SP

ISBN 1 84138 891 2

British Library Cataloguing in Publication Data
for this book is available from the British Library.

Printed in China
10 9 8 7 6 5 4 3 2 1

Acknowledgements
We wish to thank the following individuals
and organisations for their help and assistance
and for supplying material in their collections:
Alpha Archive: 8 (tl). 9 (br), 10, 13, 15 (tr),
    16 (bl), 17 (br), 18 (cl), 21 (br), 22, 25,
    27 (br), 28 (b), 29,
Gavin Page: 3, 18 (tl), 28 (tl)
John Sibbick: all other illustrations

Editorial Manager: Joyce Bentley
Design and editorial production:
Alpha Communications
Educational advisor: Julie Stapleton
Text editor: Veronica Ross

▲ The *Xiphactinus*
lived at the same time
as the last of the
dinosaurs, about 65
million years ago. See
page 10 for more
information.

Many new animals appeared later, during a period known as the 'Cambrian Explosion', and by 500 million years ago the seas were filled with wildlife. Some of these strange-looking creatures were the distant ancestors of today's animals.

▲ The *Anomalocaris* lived about 500 million years ago. The 60 cm-long hunter had feelers that stuffed prey into its circular mouth.

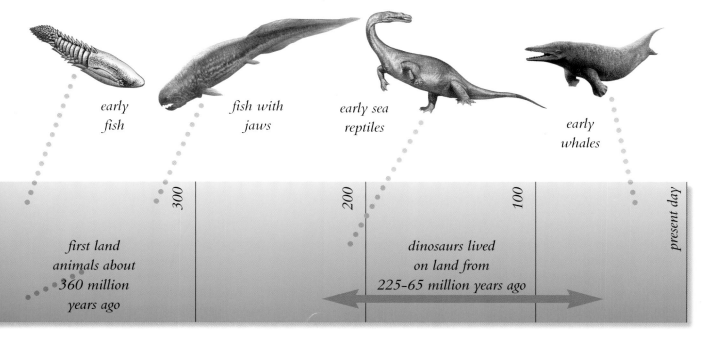

early
fish

fish with
jaws

early sea
reptiles

early
whales

300

200

100

present day

first land
animals about
360 million
years ago

dinosaurs lived
on land from
225-65 million years ago

OUTSIDE SKELETONS

Some early sea creatures looked like aliens from another planet. These were arthropods, animals with a hard outer covering instead of a backbone.

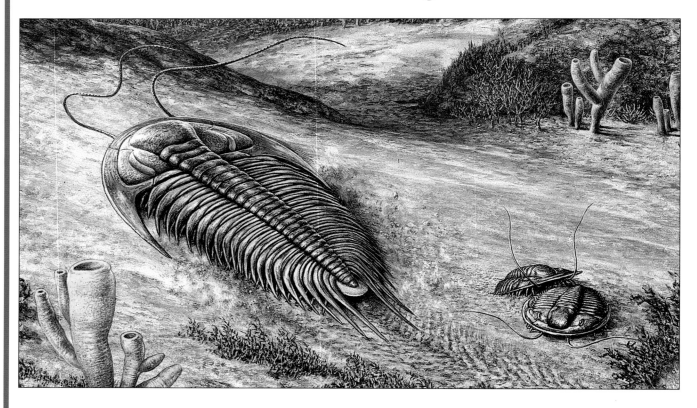

▲ Trilobites are the first known group of arthropods. They lived alongside creatures such as sea urchins, corals and shellfish.

Trilobites were arthropods that lived in the seas about 350-400 million years ago. There were more than 15 000 different kinds – some were no bigger than a pinhead, others grew more than a metre long.

Trilobites had lots of legs and used these to swim or to walk on the seabed. Trilobites were among the first animals with eyes. Like insects, trilobites had eyes made up of many separate lenses, a 'compound' eye. A human eye has just a single large lens.

flattened tail section
is called a telson

strong
claws

▲ *Eurypterus* was a fierce but small animal.
It grew only about 10 cm long.

Some arthropods looked rather like today's lobsters. One of these creatures was called the *Eurypterus*. It was a fierce killer with a long tail, strong limbs that allowed it to move quickly through the water or on the seabed, and sharp claws to grab and crush prey.

The *Pterygotus* looked quite similar but grew much larger. At 2.5m long, it was the largest arthropod there has ever been.

AMAZING ARTHROPODS

The first arthropods were among the earliest animals and are distant ancestors of modern arthropods such as crabs, lobsters, spiders and insects. Today's arthropods are the world's most widespread group of animals. There are more than a million known kinds, but all share some common features, including a hard outer casing instead of an inner skeleton. They also have jointed legs and bodies.

EARLY FISH

mouth hole

▲ Agnathan fish had a hole instead of a mouth that could open and shut.

The first fish had heads covered with bony plates. Most of them were small creatures – only a few grew more than 20 cm long.

The earliest fish are called agnathans, a word that means 'without jaws'. One of these was a little fish called the *Pteraspis*, shown below. It did not look much like fish of today, yet it had several fishlike features.

Pteraspis had a fin, although this was really a bony spine, one of several along its back. It had a head, but this was made of bony plates, like a helmet. *Pteraspis* also had a mouth, but no moving jaws – instead of biting, it sucked in tiny food particles.

▼ A scene from 400 million years ago, as jawless *Pteraspis* fish swim along looking for food, such as bits of dead plants and animals.

Pteraspis *grew about 20 cm long*

bony shield around head

eye on each side
of wide mouth

fins behind
head shield

▲ *Drepanaspis* was a
slow swimmer that
grew 30 cm long.

▶ *Hemicyclaspis* had
a body that could
bend easily.

Other fish that swam in these prehistoric seas included the
Drepanaspis and the *Hemicyclaspis*. *Drepanaspis* swam along
the muddy sea bottom, sucking up bits of food there.
The *Hemicyclaspis* was a faster swimmer with fins behind
a helmet-like head. Its body was covered with bony strips,
which let the 13 cm-long fish wriggle from side to side.

HOW DO WE KNOW
ABOUT PREHISTORIC LIFE?

Scientists find out about animals from the distant past by
studying fossils, the hardened remains of dead creatures
preserved in rock over millions of years. However, only a
few animals become fossils. Most are eaten by other animals
or decompose quickly after death. A typical fish fossil is
made when a dead fish sinks to the bottom of the sea. Sand
and silt build up over it, then minerals seep into the hard,
bony parts, changing them into rocky fossil remains.

fossil of a prehistoric sea star

MASSIVE JAWS

Moving jaws were one of the features of later fish, some of which were true sea monsters that grew to enormous sizes.

One of the first really big fish was the *Dunkleosteus*. This monster grew more than 5m long – the length of a small truck and it had jaws packed with jagged bony plates, instead of teeth. *Dunkleosteus* could probably swim fast enough to catch most other fish easily. Its razor-sharp tooth plates could slice almost any animal in half!

▶ *Dunkleosteus* lived more than 300 million years ago. Its head had a bony shield.

Xiphactinus *grew about 4m long*

fish swallowed in stomach

Later fish became more like the fish we see today. They are called teleosts ('complete bones') because they had a full skeleton with a backbone, ribs and other bones and were covered with scales. They had strong tails to drive them forwards and fins that gave precise steering. Teleosts had a swim bladder, an air-filled sac in the body that a fish uses to control its buoyancy.

THE BIG LUNCH

The *Xiphactinus* was a teleost fish that lived about 65 million years ago. It swam in the seas at about the same time as the last of the dinosaurs. Its jaws were large and low-slung, much like a present-day grouper fish. The fossilised *Xiphactinus* above may have died of overeating, because the fish it swallowed was too big to digest.

bony tooth plates

KILLER SHARKS

The earliest sharks were fierce hunters that swam in the prehistoric seas about 400 million years ago. Sharks are still deadly ocean predators today.

mouth at front of head

▲ A *Cladoselache* grew to a length of 2m.

▼ The *Stethacanthus* of 360 million years ago had an odd top fin. Its purpose is a mystery.

One of the earliest known sharks is the *Cladoselache*. This beast hunted the oceans for fish and squid about 360-400 million years ago, long before any dinosaurs walked the Earth. At first glance *Cladoselache* looks similar to a modern shark, but its mouth was at the front of its head (instead of underneath) and its snout was shorter.

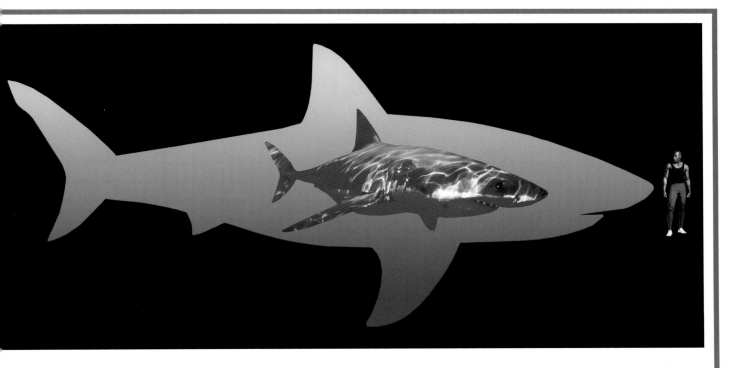

One of the biggest prehistoric sharks we know about was the huge *Carcharadon megalodon*. This monster lived about 15 million years ago and grew up to 13m long. That makes today's 6m-long Great White shark seem small!

▲ *Carcharadon megalodon* compared in size with an adult Great White shark of today, and a human.

► *Carcharadon megalodon* was a huge fish. Here a fossil tooth is shown with a tooth from a Great White shark, today's biggest hunting shark.

Great White shark tooth

Carcharadon megalodon *tooth*

GRISTLE INSTEAD OF BONE

Sharks have skeletons of gristly cartilage instead of hard bone. This makes finding shark fossils difficult because early sharks mostly rotted away in a short time. But their teeth were hard, and this made them more likely to turn into fossils. Many early sharks have been identified by checking the size and shape of their fossilised teeth.

SEA REPTILES

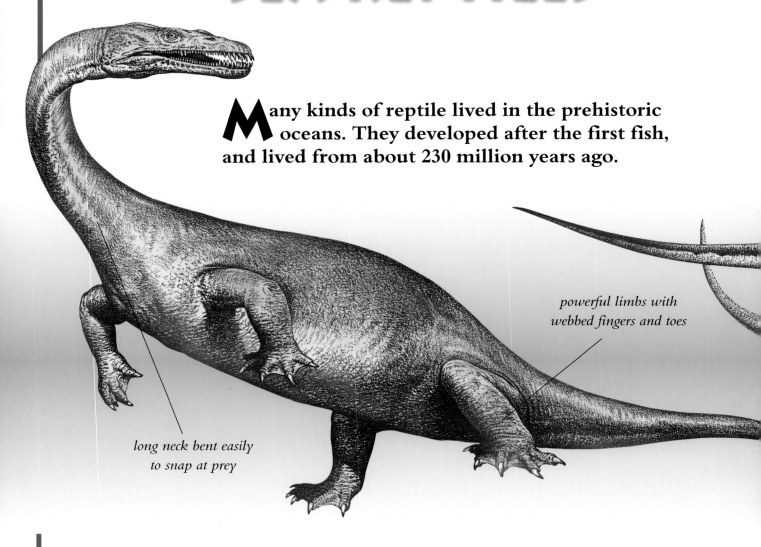

Many kinds of reptile lived in the prehistoric oceans. They developed after the first fish, and lived from about 230 million years ago.

long neck bent easily to snap at prey

powerful limbs with webbed fingers and toes

▲ There were several kinds of *Nothosaurus*. Like other sea reptiles, they breathed air not water.

Nothosaurus was a hunter that lived about 220 million years ago. It lived in the water but may also have climbed on to seashore rocks to bask in the sun. It hunted in warm, shallow waters where there were plenty of creatures to chase and eat.

Nothosaurus had long jaws that were packed with dozens of sharp teeth – just right for grabbing and hanging on to a slippery fish trying to escape.

▶ The ammonite was a favourite sea-reptile food. There were many kinds of ammonite but they all had a spiral shell, with soft inner parts and squid-like tentacles.

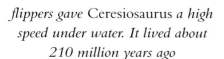

flippers gave Ceresiosaurus *a high speed under water. It lived about 210 million years ago*

Placodus was a sea reptile that lived about 200-250 million years ago. It had teeth specially-shaped for eating shellfish. *Placodus* raked up oysters with long front teeth, then crushed the shells with rounded back teeth. It chewed the tasty flesh and spat out the crunchy bits.

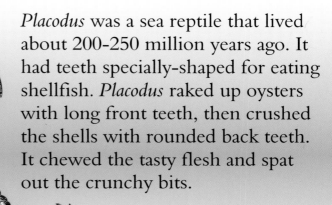

front teeth of Placodus *were shaped to scrape shellfish off rocks*

females probably laid their eggs near the shore

ammonites were common sea creatures

WHAT IS A REPTILE?

Reptiles were among the oldest animal groups to develop, and they still exist today. Reptiles breathe air and usually have a covering of scales or horny plates, rather than fur or hair. They lay tough-shelled eggs on dry land instead of giving birth to live young. They are cold-blooded, needing warm surroundings to be active.

ICHTHYOSAURS

Ichthyosaurs were reptiles, but they looked much like modern dolphins. Ichthyosaurs had long, toothed jaws that could snap up prey such as squid and fish.

Ichthyosaurs were smooth-skinned sea reptiles that swam with sweeping movements of their fins and powerful, shark-like tail. They were kings of the seas about 200 million years ago.

Their long jaws and teeth were just right for catching prey, which included various kinds of ammonite and fish. We know about their food because fossilised ichthyosaur droppings have been cut open to show food remains, including ammonite shells and fish bones.

fossil ichthyosaur set into surrounding rocks

▲ Ichthyosaurs found prey mostly by sight and smell. Their big eyes were protected by a strong ring of bones. An ichthyosaur's tail swept from side to side, like that of a fish. A dolphin's tail sweeps up and down.

There were many kinds of ichthyosaur, ranging in size from about 1m long to giants that grew to more than 20m.

WARMER WATERS OF THE PAST

Ichthyosaurs and dolphins look similar, but dolphins are sea mammals not reptiles. Their shape is about the only thing that links these animals, and even the seas that ichthyosaurs swam in were very different to those of today. Scientists believe that 150-200 million years ago, there was no ice at the North and South Poles – and seas all over the world were much warmer than now, making them a more comfortable environment for heat-loving reptiles.

dolphins have a beak and tall fin

UNDERSEA GIANTS

direction of
water flow

▲ Pliosaur nostrils had 'in' holes and 'out' holes. These allowed the pliosaur to detect scents in water as it flowed through.

O ther sea reptiles included the plesiosaurs. One group of these were the pliosaurs. These had short necks, chunky bodies and powerful flippers.

The biggest pliosaur was an underwater meat-eater that ruled the sea about 150 million years ago. *Liopleurodon* grew to more than 20m from nose to tail. It had four massive flippers that allowed it to be a fast and agile swimmer.

Liopleurodon probably hunted mostly by smell, as its nostrils were placed where sea water could flow through them. *Liopleurodon* could sniff scents in water just as land animals sniff the air for smells.

▲ A complete skeleton of *Liopleurodon* was found in Mexico in 2002. When alive, this sea monster could have weighed more than 100 tonnes.

▶ The *Liopleurodon* was long and sleek. Its skull alone measured more than 3m long.

human diver to the same scale as the main picture

the tail was too short to be used for forward thrust. The four flippers were used instead

PREHISTORIC TURTLES

Early turtles included the *Archelon*, a huge sea turtle that lived about 70-65 million years ago. It grew nearly 4m long, twice the length of any sea turtle today. *Archelon*'s big shell was made up of a framework of bony ribs, growing out from its backbone. Thick, rubbery skin grew between the ribs, forming the shield's oval shield shape.

Archelon *ate seafood such as shrimps and jellyfish*

Liopleurodon *had a bulky body, but was still very agile*

Liopleurodon used its flippers to swim, rather than wriggling its tail like a fish or an ichthyosaur. Big muscles gave a powerful downstroke, so it is likely that the flippers were used in pairs, one pair pushing down while the other pair returned for the next push.

front teeth crossed over to form a fish trap

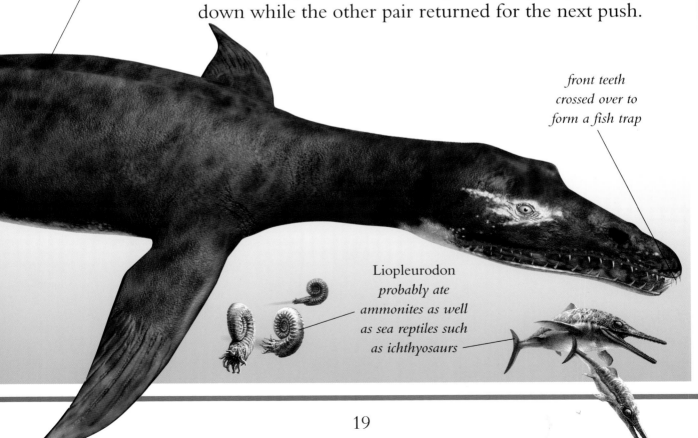

Liopleurodon *probably ate ammonites as well as sea reptiles such as ichthyosaurs*

19

LONG NECKS

Some plesiosaurs had small heads and long necks. Elasmosaurs were among the biggest of these, with necks that stretched several metres long.

Elasmosaurs are probably the best-known prehistoric sea reptiles. Their long necks had more than 70 bones and were very flexible. An elasmosaur may have fed by poking its head into a shoal of fish and sweeping its wide-open jaws from side to side, snapping up fish one after another – the bendy neck made this an easy way to go hunting. Adult elasmosaurs grew more than 14m long and swam by making powerful strokes with their pointed flippers.

A MONSTER IN LOCH NESS?

Scientists believe that plesiosaurs, along with most other sea reptiles, died out about 65 million years ago. Yet there may be the odd survivor. For hundreds of years, there have been sightings of a 'monster' swimming in Loch Ness in Scotland. Loch Ness is very long and is nearly 300m deep in places, so there may be enough room to hide a few plesiosaur-like animals.

Scientists have gone on several expeditions to try and find 'Nessie'. They have used small submarines, cameras, underwater lights and other high-tech gear, but they haven't found anything yet!

elasmosaurs hunted underwater but breathed air, like land reptiles

Not all plesiosaurs were as big as the huge elasmosaurs. For example, the *Cryptoclidus* was only about 8m long, though it still weighed 8 tonnes.

All plesiosaurs swallowed stones from the seabed. By weighing itself down with stones, a plesiosaur could hold more air in its lungs without floating to the surface. This meant it could hunt underwater for longer.

▲ Elasmosaur means 'plate lizard', after the wide, flat shoulder bones that carried the front flippers.

▼ *Cryptoclidus* was a smaller plesiosaur. Its jaws were lined with nearly 100 teeth.

SAVAGE SURVIVORS

The first crocodiles and alligators lived about 200 million years ago. However, the biggest of all time was the more recent *Deinosuchus*, which lived about 70 million years ago.

▲ A *Deinosuchus* skull is shown here to scale with a dalmatian dog. The skull measured 2m long, with jaws that were big enough to swallow most prey with a single 'snap'.

The enormous *Deinosuchus* ('terrible crocodile') was a monster that dwarfed any alligator before or since – an adult measured up to 10m long and weighed 5 tonnes.

Deinosuchus probably hunted like alligators and crocodiles do today. It floated just under the surface near the shore, waiting for an animal (such as a dinosaur) to stop for a drink. Then, coming out of the water in a surprise rush, *Deinosuchus* used its enormous jaws to seize the prey and drag it back under water to eat.

▼ *Deinosuchus*, shown to scale with the much smaller *Metriorhynchus* and a human.

Deinosuchus

Metriorhynchus

human

▲ *Deinosuchus* (far right) was big enough to snatch a dinosaur as it came to drink.

Metriorhynchus was a crocodile that lived in the sea at much the same time as *Deinosuchus*. It was smaller though, growing only about 3m long.

Metriorhynchus was not as heavily armoured as other crocodiles and had slim jaws, packed with sharp teeth that could grip wriggling fish or squid. Unusually, its tail was not pointed, instead ending in a fish-like fin.

 THE REPTILE KILLER

Almost all sea reptiles and their relatives, the dinosaurs, died out about 65 million years ago. Scientists think their deaths were caused by a changing climate and a huge meteor that struck the Earth, causing a terrible heat wave. Alligators, crocodiles and turtles are among the few sea reptiles surviving today, and alligators now live only in fresh water.

BACK TO THE SEA

There were still ocean giants after the sea reptiles had died out. These were early whales, whose ancestors had been land-dwelling mammals.

The earliest-known whale was the *Pakicetus*, but it looked very different from whales of today. It had four legs, with a separate tail and probably looked more like a seal than a whale. *Pakicetus* was not a very big whale, only growing to about 2m long. Researchers think it lived in coastal areas, where rivers met the sea about 50-55 million years ago.

▶ *Pakicetus* probably spent much of its time paddling in shallow water looking for fish to eat.

nostrils on snout

Pakicetus *was similar to a seal in shape*

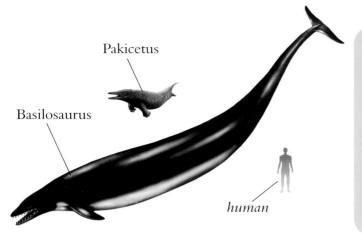

Pakicetus

Basilosaurus

human

▲ *Pakicetus, Basilosaurus* and a human to scale

ECHOLOCATION

Whales developed a 'super-sense' to help them hunt prey under water. A whale sends out powerful sound waves into the water around it. Echoes that bounce off solid objects, such as tasty fish, are received by the whale's sensitive ears, allowing it to have a 'sound-picture' of things in the water.

The *Basilosaurus* was a monster whale that came after *Pakicetus*, living about 40 million years ago. At that time the seas were filled with all sorts of animals – and *Basilosaurus* was the biggest of them all, growing over 20m long. However, *Basilosaurus* was not the only kind of mammal to go back to the sea. The distant ancestors of sea mammals familiar today, such as the seal, dugong and walrus, also once lived on land.

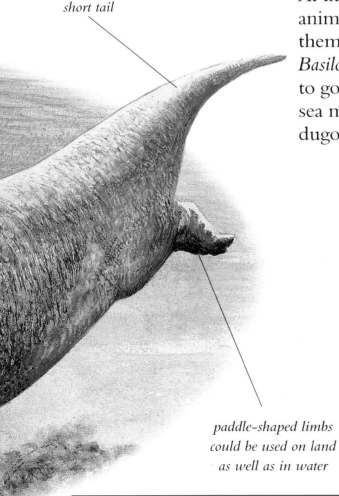

short tail

paddle-shaped limbs
could be used on land
as well as in water

▲ Today's seals live in and around water, yet they are related to land-dwelling weasels.

SEA MONSTER WORDS

◀ *Anglaspis* was a kind of agnathan fish.

Here are some technical terms used in this book.

agnathan

A general name for very early fish that had no moving jaws. There are some living kinds of agnathan, such as the lamprey.

arthropod

Animals that have a segmented body and an outer skeleton, or exoskeleton. Trilobites were prehistoric arthropods. Today, there are more than one million kinds of arthropod, including spiders and insects.

'Cambrian Explosion'

A period in the Earth's past when many new kinds of life appeared. It lasted from 540 to 500 million years ago.

cartilage

A strong but flexible material that some animals have in place of bone. A shark's skeleton is made of cartilage.

cold-blooded

An animal, such as a reptile or a fish, with blood that matches the temperature of its surroundings. After a cold night, a reptile warms up in the Sun to become active. A warm-blooded animal, such as a whale, has blood that stays at the same temperature, so the animal does not slow down in cold surroundings.

dinosaurs

A large group of four- and two-legged reptiles that lived all over the world from 225 to 65 million years ago.

fossil

The remains of a living thing preserved in rock. A 'trace' fossil preserves such things as flipper prints left in mud.

loch

Scottish word for lake.

mammal

A warm-blooded animal, such as a dolphin, whale or human. Mammals feed their young on milk from the mother's body.

meteor

Chunks of rock moving in space at high speed, ranging in size from tiny grains to flying mountains kilometres across. A big one striking the Earth is thought to have helped kill off most reptile life on the Earth about 65 million years ago.

plesiosaur

A large group of sea reptiles that had four flippers. Some kinds of plesiosaur had short necks, others had necks that were long and thin.

prey

An animal that is hunted by another animal for food. The hunter is called a predator.

reptile

An animal, such as a crocodile, that breathes air and is usually covered with scales or horny plates. Reptiles normally lay eggs with tough shells on dry land, although ichthyosaurs are thought to have given birth to live young.

skull

An animal's bony structure that contains and protects its brain, eyes, ears and nose.

swim bladder

A small sac inside a teleost fish's body that helps to control its buoyancy.

teleost

General name for fish with a bony inner skeleton. Teleosts have proved to be the most successful fish – today there are more than 20 000 kinds.

trilobite

Early arthropods that were among the first animals to have eyes. These were made of many separate lenses (like those of an insect) rather than the single lens used by fish or mammals.

WEIRD WORDS

This pronunciation guide should help you say the names of sea monsters.

Ammonite
ammo-night
Anomalocaris
a-nom-alo-car-is
Archelon
ark-el-on
Basilosaurus
bas-ill-oh-sore-rus
Carcharodon megalodon
car-char-oh-don mega-low-don
Ceresiosaurus
Ser-es-ee-oh-sore-rus
Cladoselache
clay-dos-er-lash
Cryptoclidus
krip-toe-cly-dus
Deinosuchus
dye-no-sook-us
Dickinsonia
dik-in-soh-nee-ah
Drepanaspis
drep-an-ass-pis
Dunkleosteus
dun-klee-ost-ee-us
Elasmosaur
el-az-moe-sore
Eurypterus
yer-ip-ter-rus
Hemicyclaspis
hem-ee-sigh-clasp-iss
Ichthyosaur
ik-thee-oh-sore

Liopleurodon
lie-pler-oh-don
Mawsonites
more-son-eye-teez
Metriorhynchus
met-ree-oh-rink-us
Nautiloid
nortil-oy-d
Nothosaurus
no-tho-sore-rus
Opthalmosaurus
op-thal-moe-sore-rus
Pakicetus
pak-ee-see-tus
Placodus
plah-co-dus
Plesiosaur
ples-ee-oh-sore
Pliosaur
ply-oh-sore
Pteraspis
tear-as-pis
Pterygotus
terry-goat-us
Stethacanthus
steth-ah-kan-thus
Temnodontosaurus
tem-no-don-toe-sore-rus
Trilobite
try-low-bite
Xiphactinus
zif-act-in-us

▼ Fossil remains of two small plesiosaurs.

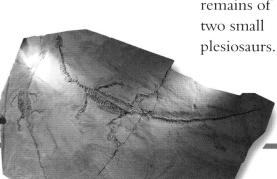

SEA MONSTER FACTS

Here are some facts and stories about strange sea creatures.

▲ Three kinds
of strange early shark.

Strange sharks

Some early sharks were truly weird. One had tentacles that grew above its eyes. Another had a forward-facing bony spine above its head, while a third kind had a bony spike growing behind its skull.

▶ *Opthalmosaurus* grew about 5m long and weighed about a tonne when fully grown.

Fighter jet or airliner?

Researchers have found that short-necked plesiosaurs had wide, stout flippers similar to a fighter plane's wings. This made them very agile and good at chasing fish. Long-necked plesiosaurs had long, slim flippers, like the wings of an airliner, making them suitable for cruising. So it's likely that long-necked plesiosaurs swam slowly over long distances, looking for prey that was easy to catch.

What big eyes you've got

The *Opthalmosaurus* was a common kind of ichthyosaur that had very large eyes. But the eyes of *Temnodontosaurus* were even bigger – one of its fossilized eyes was 264 mm across – that's the size of a dinner plate! All the many kinds of ichthyosaur had eyes that were surrounded by a 'doughnut' of bone, called the sclerotic ring. This protected the soft eyeballs when diving into the deep oceans hunting for squid.

A modern ammonite?

The ammonites died out about 65 million years ago, but the similar-looking nautilus did manage to survive. It is a rare creature that lives today in the Pacific Ocean.

First finds

Ichthyosaurs and plesiosaurs have been studied for a long time. Remains were found in Britain over 300 years ago, and drawings of a bone had been made even earlier, in 1604. A complete ichthyosaur skeleton was found much later, in 1719 and was thought for many years to be the remains of a kind of weird 'sea dragon'.

Bringing up baby

Female ichthyosaur remains have been found that seem to show they had special places to give birth to young, which were born live, rather than as eggs, like other reptiles. An ichthyosaur mother could give birth to ten or more live young at a time, though two to three were more common. Babies

▲ Mary Anning was one of the first people to dig up plesiosaur fossils, in England. In 1810 she found her first ichthyosaur, when she was just 11 years old.

were born tail-first and were about 50 cm long, making them tasty snacks for hungry sharks nearby. The birth places may have been guarded by larger male ichthyosaurs.

SEA MONSTERS SUMMARY

The first life began in the seas about 3500 million years ago. Remains found in Australia show that about 680 million years ago, jellyfish and worms were living in the water.

After the earliest sea animals, new creatures developed during a period about 500 million years ago, called the 'Cambrian Explosion'. Arthropods had hard, outer shells instead of skeletons inside their bodies. Early fish, called agnathans, had armoured heads and fixed jaws. Later fish, called teleosts, had opening jaws, as well as scales and fins. Reptiles lived in the seas for millions of years, but mostly died out about 65 million years ago, at the same time as the dinosaurs. After this, some land mammals, such as the ancestors of the whale, went to live in the sea.

▼ This 5m-long sea monster is a nautiloid that lived in the seas 400 million years ago. Some nautiloids grew up to 100 tentacles that grabbed at prey such as Trilobites.

SEA MONSTERS ON THE WEB

You can find out about prehistoric sea creatures on the Internet. Use a search engine or type in the name of the animal you want to find out about or the prehistoric period you are interested in. Here are some good sites to start with:

▼ There are good sites that have information on prehistoric sea creatures. Here are three screenshots.

http://www.oceansofkansas.com
The US state of Kansas once lay under the sea, and this fascinating site tells you all about life at that time, as well as other interesting facts.

http://www.museum.vic.gov.au/prehistoric
From ammonites to trilobites, they are all featured on this excellent Australian site.

http://www.sdsc.edu/ScienceWomen
This site features women who have made their names in science, including Mary Anning, the English Victorian-period fossil-hunter.

http://www.lymeregis.com/lymefossilshop
Want to buy a fossil? Visit this site to see a treasure trove of bits and pieces for sale.

http://www.bbc.co.uk/dinosaurs
This provides information on the TV series, *Walking with Dinosaurs*. It also has material on all sorts of prehistoric sea creatures.

INDEX